Before and After Disasters

Federal Funding for Cultural Institutions

FEMA 533/September 2005

 **FEMA**   Heritage Preservation

NATIONAL
ENDOWMENT
FOR THE ARTS

Contents

On the cover:

The Ft. Pickens Visitors Center, a historic structure housing a library, offices, and exhibits, was devastated when Hurricane Ivan struck the Gulf Islands National Seashore in 2004. The building was pushed off its foundation and broke in two.

Photo – Service Museum Resource Center

Introduction

Floods, hurricanes, and other disasters can strike with little warning and damage or destroy irreplaceable art, artifacts, books, and historic records. But there are ways to prepare for emergencies and minimize the damage they inflict. Since the events of September 11, 2001, effective emergency management has become a higher priority for the cultural community. More institutions are interested in developing disaster plans, providing staff training, and better protecting their collections. Numerous federal programs now support such important efforts. *Before and After Disasters: Federal Funding for Cultural Institutions* is designed to help archives, arts centers, libraries, museums, historical societies, and historic sites find the resources they need.

This guide is an updated and expanded version of *Resources for Recovery: Post-Disaster Aid for Cultural Institutions*, first developed in 1992 by Heritage Preservation and then revised in 2000. *Before and After Disasters* includes summary descriptions and contact information for 15 federal grant and loan programs – almost double the number of resources in the previous edition. It covers sources of federal assistance for preparedness, mitigation, and response, as well as for recovery. Sample projects in disaster planning, training, treatment research, and restoration illustrate the funding guidelines.

Before and After Disasters: Federal Funding for Cultural Institutions is an initiative of the Heritage Emergency National Task Force. It was written and produced by Heritage Preservation with funding from, and in partnership with, the Federal Emergency Management Agency and the National Endowment for the Arts as a service to the American cultural community.

Heritage Preservation

Summer 2005

About this Guide

Grant and loan guidelines are organized by agency in two sections of *Before and After Disasters*. The first section discusses financial resources for preparedness and mitigation; the second, programs for response and recovery. Each agency profile contains a general overview of the grant or loan programs, a list of eligible activities, the award amount or loan terms, and a sample project. Web site addresses are provided for additional details on application guidelines. Regional offices are listed for two agencies.

Before and After Disasters also features on-line resources for professional preservation advice that can benefit institutions and the communities they serve. Please visit the Web site of the Heritage Emergency National Task Force (*www.heritageemergency.org*) for updated links.

The following agencies have contributed to this guide:

The **Federal Emergency Management Agency (FEMA) of** the Department of Homeland Security leads America to prepare for, prevent, respond to, and recover from disasters. This mission is accomplished by reducing loss of life and property, minimizing suffering and disruption caused by disasters, preparing the nation to address the consequences of terrorism, and serving as the nation's portal for emergency management information and expertise.

The **Institute of Museum and Library Services (IMLS)** is an independent federal grant-making agency dedicated to helping the nation's 15,000 museums and 122,000 libraries serve their communities. By supporting libraries and museums, IMLS fosters leadership, innovation, and education.

The **National Center for Preservation Technology and Training (NCPTT)** is a research and education center of the National Park Service. NCPTT advances the use of technology in the fields of historic preservation, archaeology, architecture, landscape architecture, and materials conservation through training, education, research, technology transfer, and partnerships.

The **National Endowment for the Arts (NEA)** is an independent federal agency dedicated to supporting excellence in the arts, both new and established; bringing the arts to all Americans; and providing leadership in arts education.

The **National Endowment for the Humanities (NEH)** is an independent federal grant-making agency dedicated to supporting research, education, preservation, and public programs in the humanities.

The **National Historical Publications and Records Commission (NHPRC)** promotes the preservation and use of America's documentary heritage that is essential to understanding our democracy, history, and culture.

The **National Science Foundation (NSF)** is an independent federal agency with a mission to promote the progress of science; to advance the national health, prosperity, and welfare; and to secure the national defense.

The **Small Business Administration (SBA)** maintains and strengthens the nation's economy by aiding, counseling, assisting, and protecting the interests of small businesses and by helping families and businesses recover from natural disasters. In the wake of disasters, the SBA provides loans to help nonprofit organizations, businesses of all sizes, and homeowners and renters with long-term recovery efforts.

DISASTER MANAGEMENT DEFINITIONS

Preparedness means being ready to handle disasters and emergencies. Risk assessments, disaster planning, adequate supplies, trained staff, and community partnerships all contribute to disaster preparedness.

Mitigation is the process of preventing or minimizing the losses and damages that emergencies can cause.

Response involves actions taken to deal with a disaster or emergency. Response is about the emergency itself, as well as the problems it creates.

Recovery means restoring services, facilities, programs, collections, and infrastructure.

Resources for Preparedness and Mitigation

Effective emergency preparedness is essential if cultural institutions and heritage sites are to rapidly respond when facilities and collections are threatened by disasters. It is equally important that institutions and sites look for opportunities to reduce future disaster damages by implementing hazard mitigation measures. The following funding sources can support preparedness and mitigation activities.

This Missouri Post Office was submerged by flood waters in July 1993. High water levels can move even the heaviest objects and leave rooms in shambles.
Photo by Andrea Booher/FEMA Photo.

FEDERAL BUILDING
UNITED STATES POST OFFICE

Federal Emergency Management Agency

The **Pre-Disaster Mitigation (PDM) Program** assists states, Indian tribes, and local governments with cost-effective hazard mitigation activities that complement a comprehensive mitigation program. The PDM Program provides a significant opportunity before disasters strike to raise risk awareness and reduce disaster losses through planning and project grants. Eligible applicants are state emergency management agencies or similar offices of a state, the District of Columbia, the U.S. Virgin Islands, Puerto Rico, Guam, and the Pacific Territories, as well as federally recognized Indian tribal governments. State-level agencies, state-recognized Indian tribes and federally recognized Indian tribal governments, local governments, and public colleges and universities are eligible for funding as sub-applicants and must apply through eligible applicants to receive PDM Program funds. Private nonprofit organizations and institutions are not eligible sub-applicants; however, relevant state agencies or local governments may apply for assistance on their behalf.

Eligible Activities:	PDM Program funds must be used for hazard mitigation planning and/or the implementation of mitigation projects prior to a disaster. Eligible mitigation plans and projects must be long-term, feasible, and cost-effective.
Award Amounts:	Funding is restricted to a maximum of $3 million federal share per planning or per project sub-application and is subject to a 75 percent federal/25 percent non-federal cost share. The non-federal match does not need to be cash; in-kind services or materials may be used. PDM funds are available until expended and are awarded on a competitive basis without state allocations or quotas.
Additional Information:	Visit *www.fema.gov/fima/pdm* for updated information and the next application period. Eligibility requirements for private nonprofits can be found at *www.fema.gov/txt/fima/pnp_fact_sheet.txt*.

The **Hazard Mitigation Grant Program (HMGP)** provides assistance to implement long-term hazard mitigation measures after major disaster declarations. The purpose of the program is to reduce property loss due to natural disasters and to enable mitigation measures to be implemented during the immediate recovery from a disaster. HMGP funding is only available to applicants within a designated disaster area. State and local governments, Indian tribes or other tribal organizations, and eligible private nonprofit organizations or institutions that own or operate private nonprofit facilities can apply for HMGP funding through their state emergency management agency. Eligible private nonprofit facilities include museums, zoos, and libraries.

Eligible Activities: HMGP funds may be used to support projects that will reduce or eliminate losses from future disasters. Eligible projects provide a long-term solution to a problem—for example, the elevation of a structure to reduce the risk of future flood damage as opposed to the purchase of sandbags and pumps to fight the flood. A project's potential savings must be more than the cost of implementing the project. HMGP funds may be used to protect either public or private property or to purchase property that has been subjected to, or is in danger of, repetitive damage.

Award Amounts: Award amounts vary and are subject to a 75 percent federal/25 percent non-federal cost share. The non-federal match does not need to be cash; in-kind services or materials may be used. The state prioritizes and selects project applications developed and submitted by local jurisdictions and forwards applications consistent with state and local mitigation planning objectives to FEMA for eligibility review. Funding for this program is limited to 7.5 percent of the total grants awarded by FEMA in a disaster.

Sample Project: Following the 1989 Loma Prieta earthquake, the City of San Francisco received HMGP funding for the seismic retrofit of the San Francisco City Hall, one of the finest examples of classical architecture in the United States and a National Historic Landmark. During the retrofit, the building's foundation was separated from the earth around it to protect both the occupants and historic architecture from future earthquakes. It is now the largest base-isolated building in the world.

Additional Information: Visit www.fema.gov/fima/hmgp.

Institute of Museum and Library Services

The **Conservation Project Support (CPS) Program** awards grants to help museums identify conservation needs and priorities to ensure the safekeeping of their living and nonliving collections. A proposed project must be a top institutional collections care priority and meet the institution's highest conservation needs. Applicants must demonstrate that the primary goal of the project is conservation care and not collections management or maintenance.

Eligible Activities:	Grants are available for five broad types of conservation activities including surveys (general, detailed condition, or environmental), training, research, treatment, and environmental improvements. Collections may be nonliving, natural history, living plants, or living animals.
Award Amounts:	Awards are limited to $150,000. Exceptional projects can be awarded up to $250,000. An institution may submit one application each fiscal year. Applicants may also receive up to $10,000 to develop an educational component that directly relates to their project.
Sample Projects:	The Arizona State Museum (Tempe, Arizona) received a $22,423 CPS program award to conduct planning and staff training leading to the development of a disaster preparedness and recovery plan. The Oakland Museum (Oakland, California) received $24,965 to improve environmental conditions in the collections storage area with special attention to earthquake mitigation measures.
Additional Information:	Contact the Senior Program Officer in the Office of Museum Services at (202) 653-4641 or visit *www.imls.gov/grants/museum/index.htm.* Sample application narratives are available on-line.

Through the Library Services and Technology Act (LSTA), the IMLS Office of Library Services distributes **Grants to State Library Agencies** using a population-based formula. State and territorial library agencies may use these funds to support statewide initiatives and services. LSTA appropriations awarded to library agencies may also be used for subgrant competitions or cooperative agreements to public, academic, research, school, and special libraries.

Eligible Activities:	Grants to State Library Agencies can support projects that use technology for information sharing between libraries as well as between libraries and other community services and to support projects that make library resources more accessible to urban, rural, or low-income residents. Each state or territorial library agency develops its own spending plan. Several states have used LSTA funds to award subgrants for projects that include disaster planning.
Award Amounts:	Award amounts vary. Each state or territory develops its own plan for spending the funds.
Sample Project:	The Washington State Library (Olympia, Washington) used an IMLS Grant to State Library Agencies to launch the Washington Preservation Initiative, which has three objectives: to preserve historical library collections in all formats, to give citizens access to collections, and to help library staff develop preservation expertise. The Washington Preservation Initiative sponsored a workshop series that included training on disaster planning.
Additional Information:	For more information visit *www.imls.gov/grants/library/index.htm.*

The IMLS **National Leadership Grants** program in the Office of Library Services supports research and demonstration projects to improve library services. Funding is awarded to projects that have a national impact and provide models that can be widely adapted or replicated by others. IMLS establishes a set of priorities each fiscal year and gives funding preference to projects that address them.

Eligible Activities: The National Leadership Grants program supports model projects to improve library services, including collections care and disaster planning. All types of libraries, except federal and for-profit libraries, are eligible to apply. Other eligible entities include library associations, library consortia, and institutions of higher learning. Library applicants may apply individually or as partners with organizations such as museums, archives, and other cultural heritage organizations.

Award Amounts: Grant amounts range from $25,000 to $1 million with a 1:1 match required for requests over $250,000 and cost sharing of at least 1/3 encouraged for requests under $250,000 and for research projects.

Sample Project: The Northeast Document Conservation Center in partnership with the Massachusetts Board of Library Commissioners received a National Leadership Grant to develop and disseminate an on-line training tool to help librarians write disaster plans. The partners will also develop a training curriculum for smaller libraries and museums entitled "Steal This Disaster Plan."

Additional Information: To learn more or see a current list of program priorities visit *www.imls.gov/grants/library/index.htm*.

National Center for Preservation Technology and Training

Preservation Technology and Training Grants support research, training, meetings, conferences, and publications that further the Center's mission. Preference is given to research and training projects that protect cultural resources against vandalism, looting, terrorism, and natural disasters; conserve architectural materials of the "recent past"; develop appropriate technologies to preserve houses of worship and cemeteries; monitor and evaluate preservation treatments; study environmental effects of pollution on cultural resources; and document and preserve threatened cultural landscapes.

Eligible Activities:	Preservation Technology and Training Grants may be used to fund projects that protect cultural resources against vandalism, looting, terrorism, and natural disasters and projects that develop preservation technologies to assist with preparedness, prevention, and recovery. NCPTT supports single-year projects.
Award Amounts:	Grants are awarded competitively with a maximum award of $40,000.
Sample Project:	The University of Utah (Salt Lake City, Utah) received a Preservation Technology and Training Grant for a project entitled "Protocol for Emergency Washing, Drying, and Sterilization of Historically Significant Books." The project examined the long-term physical effects from commonly used techniques. The study's outcomes will allow disaster response professionals to define optimal recovery protocols based on collection age and historic value, predominant paper types, and institutional budgetary constraints.
Additional Information:	Visit www.ncptt.nps.gov or contact the Environmental and Materials Research Program Manager at (318) 356-7444.

National Endowment for the Arts

Although the NEA does not receive special appropriations to support disaster relief activities, the Endowment may provide financial support to public arts agencies and arts organizations for disaster preparedness and prevention activities that may arise out of natural disasters or terrorist acts. The NEA provides funding for projects involving the presentation, performance, exhibition, creation, preservation and conservation of art and for arts education in the fields of dance, design, folk and traditional arts, local arts agencies, literature, media arts, museums, music, musical theater, opera, presenting, theater, and visual arts.

Grants for Arts Projects are awarded through three categories—Access to Artistic Excellence, Challenge America: Reaching Every Community Fast-Track Review Grants, and Learning in the Arts for Children and Youth.

Eligible Activities: An applicant organization must be a 501(c)(3) nonprofit, tax-exempt organization with a three-year history of arts programming. The NEA provides matching grants on a competitive basis for projects of national, regional, or field-wide significance. This includes projects that can serve as models for a field or have significant effects within communities. Projects related to disaster preparedness and mitigation are eligible for support.

Award Amounts: Award amounts vary according to category and are limited to $150,000. The average size of an NEA grant is $25,000.

Sample Projects: The Craft Emergency Relief Fund (Montpelier, Vermont) received a $15,000 grant to add disaster prevention information to the Fund's Web site for craft artists. The site, which currently provides information to any professional craft artist experiencing career-threatening illness, accident, fire, theft, or natural disaster, will be expanded to include a clearinghouse of information and resources on business planning, risk management, health and safety resources, and disaster prevention. Architecture for Humanity (New York, New York) received a $15,000 grant to support the design and planning of emergency shelter sites. The project involved an international design competition and workshop with architects, designers, and relief professionals to establish a set of "best practice" principles for improving emergency shelters and camps.

Additional Information: Visit *www.arts.gov/grants/apply* or contact *webmgr@arts.gov.*

At the Gulf Islands National Seashore, recovery workers pack up damaged objects in specially designed crates. Federal funding is available for essential disaster supplies.

Photo courtesy the National Park Service Museum Resource Center.

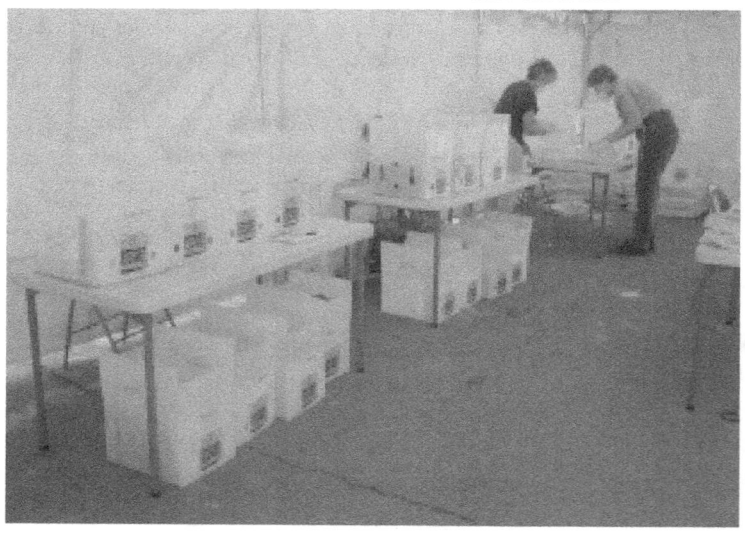

National Endowment for the Humanities

The Division of Preservation and Access provides leadership and support to preserve humanities collections in America's libraries, museums, archives, and historical organizations. **Preservation Education and Training Grants** support national or regional projects that focus on the development and presentation of courses or programs on the care and management of humanities collections for staff in cultural organizations.

Eligible Activities: Preservation Education and Training Grants may be used to fund training programs that focus on disaster preparedness or mitigation or that use it as a component part. Regional preservation field services that include disaster preparedness and response assistance among their services are also eligible in this category.

Award Amounts: Preservation Education and Training Grants are two-year awards and have ranged from $50,000 to $600,000. NEH support will not exceed 80 percent of a project's total eligible costs.

Sample Project: Disaster assistance and preparedness services are offered by NEH-supported regional field service programs. For example, the Upper Midwest Conservation Association received NEH funding for its field service program, which assists cultural heritage repositories in the Upper Midwest through educational workshops, general needs assessment surveys and collection-specific surveys, and a mentoring program and technical assistance. The program is also available during business hours to give immediate assistance with disaster recovery efforts.

Additional Information: Eligibility requirements, application guidelines, and deadlines are available at *www.neh.gov*.

The Division of Preservation and Access provides **Preservation Assistance Grants for Smaller Institutions** to help institutions improve their ability to preserve and care for their humanities collections. These institutions include libraries, museums, historical societies, archival repositories, town and county records offices, and underserved departments and units within colleges and universities.

Eligible Activities:	Preservation Assistance Grants for Smaller Institutions support activities such as general preservation assessments; consultations with professionals to address a specific preservation need, which might include developing disaster preparedness and response plans; purchase of storage furniture and preservation supplies; and preservation workshops, which can focus on disaster preparedness and response.
Award Amounts:	Preservation Assistance Grants for Smaller Institutions are up to $5,000.
Sample Projects:	The Sweetwater County Historical Museum (Green River, Wyoming) received a $5,000 Preservation Assistance Grant for Smaller Institutions to have a consultant provide disaster preparedness and response training for staff and volunteers at the museum and neighboring cultural institutions. The Southern Ute Cultural Center and Museum (Ignacio, Colorado) received $4,730 to complete a response and recovery plan with the help of a preservation consultant and to hold an on-site emergency preparedness workshop. Pikeville College (Pikeville, Kentucky) received $3,325 to purchase preservation supplies, including disaster response materials, that were recommended by a preservation consultant.
Additional Information:	Eligibility requirements, application guidelines, and deadlines are available at *www.neh.gov*.

National Historical Publications and Records Commission

NHPRC Grants support projects to preserve, publish, and encourage the use of documentary sources. Statewide programs relating to disaster preparedness or mitigation may be supported through grants made to State Historical Records Advisory Boards. Activities relating to disaster preparedness or mitigation are also eligible for NHPRC Grants under the category of Preserving and Providing Access to Records. Under this category, the Commission supports projects that help archives, colleges and universities, and historical societies assess records conditions and needs, develop archival and records management programs, and provide support for preserving and microfilming historical photographs, newsfilms, and sound recordings.

Eligible Activities: Examples of eligible activities are disaster preparedness or mitigation planning for individual archival institutions or other historical records repositories as part of an archives and records program, planning for consortia on a statewide basis, and the development or provision of educational opportunities for archives or historical records custodians.

Award Amounts: There is no set limit on grant amounts, but the majority fall in the $5,000 to $200,000 range.

Sample Projects: A grant to the Florida Department of State Division of Library and Information Services (Tallahassee, Florida) awarded $38,060 to the Florida State Historical Records Advisory Board to provide disaster planning and recovery training and to establish a consortium to coordinate statewide efforts to address disaster and disaster recovery issues. The New York State Archives State Education Department (Albany, New York) awarded $289,613 to the New York State Historical Records Advisory Board to help support a project to carry out documentation and records arrangement and description projects addressing the World Trade Center disaster and its impact on New Yorkers and

other under-documented groups, topics, and
activities in the state.

Additional Information: Contact the Director of State Programs at
(202) 501-5610 or nhprc@nara.gov or visit
www.archives.gov/grants.

On October 30, 2004, the
University of Hawaii at Manoa
Hamilton Library was hit by a
flash flood. A wall of water
carrying mud and debris crashed
through the ground floor, leaving
only load-bearing walls standing.
Mold was a major problem.
Photo: Susan Murata

National Science Foundation

The National Science Foundation, through its **Biological Research Collections (BRC) Program**, provides support for biological collection enhancement, computerization of specimen-related data, research to develop better methods for specimen curation and collection management, and activities such as symposia and workshops to investigate support and management of biological collections.

Eligible Activities: The BRC Program may support activities related to disaster preparedness and prevention. For example, the BRC Program has provided funding for earthquake-resistant cabinets and supported emergency preparedness and prevention workshops.

Award Amounts: The maximum budget that can be requested from the NSF is $500,000 per award.

Sample Project: The BRC Program funded a workshop during the annual meeting of the Society for the Preservation of Natural History Collections (SPNHC) entitled "Workshop on Emergency Preparedness, Response, and Salvage in Natural History Collections." The meeting featured presentations on preparedness and response in the context of institution-, city-, and nationwide events. The workshop aimed to educate a wide variety of museum professionals about the challenges and collaborative efforts required when writing an emergency response and salvage plan.

Additional Information: For program guidelines visit *www.nsf.gov/bio/dbi/about.jsp* or contact the Biological Research Collections Program Officer at (703) 292-8470 or dbibrc@nsf.gov.

Resources for Response and Recovery

Disasters can occur at any time and without warning, so it is best to know the options in advance. The following federal resources can help cultural institutions in response and recovery efforts. This section also explains how the federal emergency assistance system works and gives disaster response tips to help you get started.

About 3,000 photographs had to be rinsed and dried after the flash flood at the University of Hawaii at Manoa. Volunteers stepped in to help with the massive job.

Photo: Susan Murata

How the System Works

State and local emergency managers are the first line of defense. You can find a list of state agencies on FEMA's Web site at *www.fema.gov/fema/statedr.shtm*.

When a disaster exceeds the capabilities of local and state resources, the state turns to the federal government for help. The governor requests that the President of the United States declare a "major disaster" or an "emergency" to implement the National Response Plan and make available federal disaster assistance. This assistance supplements the efforts and available resources of state and local governments, voluntary relief organizations, and other forms of assistance such as insurance. Federal disaster assistance is available only if the President declares a major disaster.

After the President declares a major disaster or emergency, FEMA designates the geographic area, usually counties or other political subdivisions, eligible for disaster assistance and the types of assistance available. FEMA then establishes a temporary Joint Field Office within the affected area to coordinate the disaster relief and recovery effort.

If the damages are less extensive, the governor may ask the Administrator of the Small Business Administration (SBA) for an SBA declaration rather than a Presidential one.

First Steps: Disaster Response Tips

Coordinating the needs of salvage and financial recovery may seem overwhelming in the first days after a disaster. The following tips can help you respond effectively under stressful circumstances.

- Keep personnel off-site until state or local officials inspect for major safety threats such as structural damage, contamination, fallen electrical wires, and gas leaks.
- Inform local emergency management officials of the damage to your institution.
- Contact your insurance agent immediately.
- Check local media for contact numbers for technical and financial disaster assistance.
- Locate the original or obtain the off-site copy of your emergency plan, collection inventory, financial records, and insurance policy.

- Assess the damage as soon as you can re-enter the building. Document the damage in writing and with videotape and/or photographs.
- Begin cleanup and salvage as soon as possible. Don't wait for the insurance agent or adjuster, but remember to fully document the damage before recovery efforts begin.
- Do not throw away damaged items; they may be salvageable. Items that cannot be salvaged should be kept as proof of loss. Isolate contaminated objects.

In March 2004, the storage facility of the New Mexico Museum of Indian Arts and Culture's Archaeological Research Collections in Santa Fe was flooded by a hot water pipe that broke and flowed unchecked for almost 24 hours. Approximately 1,400 boxes were immersed in water, and objects inside them had to be removed and dried.

Museum of Indian Arts and Culture/Laboratory of Anthropology, Department of Cultural Affairs *www.miaclab.*

Photo: Anthony Thibodeau

Federal Emergency Management Agency

The **Public Assistance Program** provides supplemental federal disaster grant assistance for the repair, replacement, or restoration of facilities damaged in Presidentially declared disasters. Eligible applicants include states, Indian tribes, local governments, and certain private nonprofit organizations and institutions. These eligible private nonprofit organizations and institutions must own or operate facilities that provide educational, utility, medical, custodial care, or other essential governmental type services to the general public. Private nonprofit organizations that do not provide a critical service (power, water, sewer, wastewater treatment, communications, and emergency medical care) must first apply for a loan from the Small Business Administration (SBA) for permanent repair or restoration costs. If the SBA declines the organization's application for a loan or the disaster damages exceed the maximum amount of the SBA loan, the organization then may apply to FEMA for assistance.

For the purpose of Public Assistance funding, the FEMA Museum Eligibility Policy defines private nonprofit museums as confined facilities that are constructed or manufactured whose primary purposes are to preserve documented collections of artistic, historic, scientific, or other objects, and to exhibit the documented collections to the general public.

In addition, the FEMA Collections and Individual Objects Policy states that funding may be available for damaged collections and objects of eligible public or private nonprofit facilities when the collections are of exceptionally significant cultural value, accessible to the general public for educational purposes, and accessioned and catalogued and/or inventoried.

Eligible Activities:	To be eligible, repair, replacement, or restoration projects must be required as the result of a declared disaster, be located within a designated disaster area, and be the legal responsibility of an eligible applicant. While equipment and furnishings of facilities are eligible for replacement, objects considered under the Collections Policy are eligible only for repair.
Award Amounts:	Award amounts vary and are typically subject to a 75 percent federal/25 percent non-federal cost share.

Sample Project: The Baltimore Museum of Industry (Baltimore, Maryland) received FEMA Public Assistance funding following Hurricane Isabel in 2003. The museum, located on the city's Inner Harbor, suffered extensive storm damage. Collections held in a basement storage area were inundated by sewage that backed up to a depth of five feet. Following the Presidential disaster declaration, the museum, a private nonprofit institution, applied for federal disaster assistance. Anticipated damages exceeded the maximum level of SBA loan assistance, and the museum qualified for FEMA Public Assistance funding. FEMA determined that the museum collection was of exceptionally significant cultural value and had been legally conveyed and properly accessioned, and therefore was eligible for assistance. Conservators worked with museum staff to prepare a stabilization and treatment plan for the salvageable objects, and the collection is now stored in a newly refurbished facility.

Additional Information: Visit www.fema.gov/rrr/pa for information on applicant eligibility, project eligibility, project requirements, and the application process. The FEMA Museum Eligibility Policy (www.fema.gov/rrr/pa/9521_2.shtm) clarifies what constitutes an eligible private nonprofit museum. The Collections and Individual Objects Policy (www.fema.gov/rrr/pa/9524_6.shtm) describes Public Assistance funding eligibility criteria for damaged cultural collections.

National Endowment for the Arts

While the NEA does not receive special appropriations to support disaster relief activities, the Chairman may award **Extraordinary Action** grants in response to emergency situations. These grants are made only when extraordinary circumstances merit immediate attention and warrant bypassing the customary review process. Recipients must meet the same eligibility requirements stated in the NEA guidelines. Organizations may also apply under **Grants for Arts Projects** on the timeline specified in the guidelines.

Eligible Activities: Extraordinary Action grants may be awarded to replace costumes, sets, props, or supplies; restore damaged art collections; or help support arts programs that will allow the affected organization and community to address the disaster.

Award Amounts: Grant amounts are up to $30,000. They may be matching or non-matching at the discretion of the Chairman.

Sample Projects: Following Hurricane Charley, the Orlando Ballet (Orlando, Florida) received a $10,000 grant for the repair and restoration of costumes, sets, and props; the replacement of office furniture; and interior air cleanup. A grant of $10,000 was awarded to the Arts & Humanities Council of Charlotte County (Port Charlotte, Florida) to help artists and cultural organizations replace art, studio space, and supplies destroyed by the hurricane.

Additional Information: Visit www.arts.gov/grants/apply (Grants for Arts Projects) or contact webmgr@arts.gov.

National Endowment for the Humanities

NEH Emergency Grants are made only when extraordinary circumstances merit immediate attention and warrant bypassing the customary review process. In the aftermath of a disaster, Emergency Grants may be awarded to salvage or protect humanities collections when assistance from FEMA is not available. The NEH provides most of its support for disaster response and recovery through grants to regional field service programs. Before submitting a request for an Emergency Grant, applicants must contact the Division of Preservation and Access to ensure the availability of funds and the eligibility of the request.

Eligible Activities: Emergency Grants may be awarded to salvage or protect humanities collections when assistance from FEMA is not available.

Award Amounts: Grants are up to $30,000.

Sample Projects: The Hot Spring County Library (Malvern, Arkansas) received an NEH Emergency Grant of $18,966 to salvage books on Arkansas history and literature damaged after a fire. The American Royal Association (Kansas City, Missouri) was awarded $29,801 to extract water from its exhibition galleries and to treat collections, which had been damaged by flooding.

Additional Information: Contact the Division of Preservation and Access at (202) 606-8570 or preservation@neh.gov.

Small Business Administration

Small Business Administration **Physical Disaster Business Loans** are available to nonprofit organizations for uncompensated physical losses that are a result of declared disasters. Loans are available in areas declared a disaster by the President of the United States or the SBA Administrator after a request from the governor of the affected state. The loans have low interest rates (generally around 4 percent), long terms (up to 30 years), and refinancing of prior debts in some cases. By law, loans are offered at a higher rate of interest (8 percent maximum) for applicants that have the financial capacity to recover from the disaster without federal assistance. Over 90 percent of the SBA's disaster loans are offered at the lower rate. SBA will verify damages and estimate the cost to repair or replace the structure and its contents to pre-disaster conditions. Insurance proceeds that are required to be applied against outstanding mortgages do not reduce loan eligibility. However, any insurance proceeds voluntarily applied to outstanding mortgages do reduce the amount of eligibility.

Eligible Activities: Loan assistance is available to nonprofit organizations such as art museums, historical societies, churches, and private universities to fund repairs or replacement of disaster-damaged real estate, machinery and equipment, inventory, and other assets. Only uninsured or uncompensated disaster-related losses are eligible for loans. Disaster loans may be increased to finance mitigation measures to prevent damage in similar disasters.

Award Amounts: The maximum disaster loan available to nonprofit organizations for uncompensated disaster-related physical losses is $1.5 million. Disaster victims must repay the loans, and the SBA can only approve loans to applicants that have satisfactory credit and a reasonable ability to repay the loan.

Additional Information: Visit *www.sba.gov/disaster.*

Contact Information

Federal Emergency Management Agency (FEMA)
Environmental and Historic Preservation and Cultural Resources Programs
www.fema.gov/ehp (Web site)

FEMA Regional Offices
www.fema.gov/regions/

FEMA – Region I
99 High Street, 6th Floor
Boston, MA 02110
(617) 956-7506 (phone)
(617) 956-7519 (fax)
Serves: CT, MA, ME, NH, RI, VT

FEMA – Region II
26 Federal Plaza, Room 1307
New York, NY 10278-0002
(212) 680-3600 (phone)
(212) 680-3681 (fax)
Serves: NJ, NY, PR, VI

FEMA – Region III
One Independence Mall, 6th Floor
615 Chestnut Street
Philadelphia, PA 19106-4404
(215) 931-5608 (phone)
(215) 931-5621 (fax)
Serves: DC, DE, MD, PA, VA, WV

FEMA – Region IV
3003 Chamblee-Tucker Road
Atlanta, GA 30341-4112
(770) 220-5200 (phone)
(770) 220-5230 (fax)
Serves: AL, FL, GA, KY, MS, NC, SC, TN

FEMA – Region V
536 South Clark Street
Chicago, IL 60605-1521
(312) 408-5500 (phone)
(312) 408-5521 (fax)
Serves: IL, IN, MI, MN, OH, WI

FEMA – Region VI
Federal Regional Center
800 North Loop 288
Denton, TX 76209-3698
(940) 898-5399 (phone)
(940) 898-5325 (fax)
Serves: AR, LA, NM, OK, TX

FEMA – Region VII
2323 Grand Boulevard, Suite 900
Kansas City, MO 64108-2670
(816) 283-7061 (phone)
(816) 283-7582 (fax)
Serves: KS, MO, NE, IA

FEMA – Region VIII
Denver Federal Center
Building 710, Box 25267
Denver, CO 80225-0267
(303) 235-4800 (phone)
(303) 235-4976 (fax)
Serves: CO, MT, ND, SD, UT, WY

FEMA - Region IX
1111 Broadway, Suite 1200
Oakland, CA 94607-4052
(510) 627-7100 (phone)
(510) 627-7112 (fax)
Serves: AZ, CA, HI, NV, Pacific Territories

FEMA – Region X
Federal Regional Center
130 228th Street, SW
Bothell, WA 98021-9796
(425) 487-4600 (phone)
(425) 487-4692 (fax)
Serves: AK, ID, OR, WA

Institute of Museum and Library Services (IMLS)
1800 M Street, NW, 9th Floor
Washington, DC 20036
(202) 653-4641 (phone)
(202) 653-4608 (fax)
imlsinfo@imls.gov (e-mail)
www.imls.gov (Web site)

National Center for Preservation Technology and Training (NCPTT)
645 College Avenue
Natchitoches, LA 71457
(318) 356-7444 (phone)
(318) 356-9119 (fax)
ncptt@nps.gov (e-mail)
www.ncptt.nps.gov (Web site)

National Endowment for the Arts (NEA)
1100 Pennsylvania Avenue, NW
Washington, DC 20506
(202) 682-5400 (phone)
(202) 682-5638 (fax)
webmgr@arts.endow.gov (e-mail)
www.arts.gov (Web site)

National Endowment for the Humanities (NEH)
Division of Preservation and Access
1100 Pennsylvania Avenue, NW
Room 411
Washington, DC 20506
(202) 606-8570 (phone)
(202) 606-8639 (fax)
preservation@neh.gov (e-mail)
www.neh.gov (Web site)

National Historical Publications and Records Commission (NHPRC)
The National Archives and Records Administration (NARA)
700 Pennsylvania Avenue, NW, Room 106
Washington, DC 20408-0001
(202) 501-5610 (phone)
(202) 501-5601 (fax)
nhprc@nara.gov (e-mail)
www.archives.gov/grants (Web site)

National Science Foundation (NSF)
Biological Research Collections
NSF Division of Biological Infrastructure,
615 N
4201 Wilson Boulevard
Arlington, VA 22230
(703) 292-8470 (phone)
(703) 292-9063 (fax)
dbibrc@nsf.gov (e-mail)
www.nsf.gov (Web site)

Small Business Administration (SBA)
www.sba.gov/disaster (Web site)

SBA Offices

Disaster Area 1 Office
Small Business Administration
103 S. Elmwood Avenue
Buffalo, NY 14202
(800) 659-2955 (phone)
(716) 282-1472 (fax)
Serves: CT, DC, DE, MD, ME. MA, NH, NJ, NY, PA, RI, VA, VT, WV, PR, VI

Disaster Area 2 Office
Small Business Administration
One Baltimore Place, Suite 300
Atlanta, GA 30308
(800) 359-2227 (phone)
(404) 347-3813 (fax)
Serves: AL, FL, GA, IL, IN, KY, MI, MN, MS, NC, OH, SC, TN, WI

Disaster Area 3 Office
Small Business Administration
14925 Kingsport Road
Fort Worth, TX 76155
(800) 366-6303 (phone)
(817) 684-5616 (fax)
Serves: AR, CO, IA, KS, LA, MO, MT, ND, NE, NM, SD, OK, TX, UT, WY

Disaster Area 4 Office
P.O. Box 419004
Sacramento, CA 95841-9004
(800) 488-5323 (phone)
(916) 735-1683 (fax)
Serves: AK, AZ, CA, HI, ID, NV, OR, WA and the Pacific Territories

On-line Information

The following Web sites provide preparedness and response expertise for cultural institutions, individuals, and communities. The resources were selected by the Heritage Emergency National Task Force, which maintains the list at www.heritagepreservation.org/programs /tfc.htm. Web addresses are subject to change.

American Institute for Conservation (AIC)

www.aic-faic.org

The American Institute for Conservation of Historic and Artistic Works (AIC) is the professional membership organization for conservation professionals. The Web site provides an on-line service to help the public identify and locate professional conservation services.

AMIGOS Library Services

www.amigos.org

AMIGOS Library Services is one of the nation's largest library resource-sharing networks and is a leader in providing information technology to libraries, services libraries, and cultural institutions, primarily in the Southwest. AMIGOS provides information, guidance, and referrals to local resources, gives on-site assistance as required, and offers disaster planning workshops.

California Preservation Program

calpreservation.org

The California Preservation Program provides preservation-related resources to libraries, archives, historical societies, cultural institutions, and records repositories in California. Resources for emergency preparedness and response include the Generic Disaster Plan Workbook and the Library Disaster Plan Template, frameworks for institutions writing their own disaster plans, and the Disaster Plan Exercise, which can be used to test existing plans and help train staff.

Colorado Preservation Alliance

ahc.uwyo.edu/srma/preservation

The Colorado Preservation Alliance Web site features a disaster recovery database with recommendations on salvage procedures for a range of objects.

Conservation Center for Art and Historic Artifacts (CCAHA)

www.ccaha.org/emergency_ resource.php

A regional conservation laboratory that specializes in the treatment of art and artifacts on paper, CCAHA provides information on damaged collections, strategies for recovering from water, fire, pest infestation, or mold outbreaks, and referrals for commercial vendors and suppliers. Technical bulletins that address disaster recovery needs and an Emergency Resource Guide are available on-line.

Conservation Information Network

www.bcin.ca

BCIN, the Bibliographic Database of the Conservation Information Network, is a bibliographic resource for the conservation, preservation, and restoration of cultural property. Users can search for papers and resource materials on emergency response and preparedness.

Conservation OnLine (CoOL)

palimpsest.stanford.edu/bytopic/disasters

CoOL is a full text library of conservation information, covering a wide spectrum of topics related to the conservation of library, archive, and museum materials. The section on disaster planning and response includes disaster plans, case histories, and other resources with Web links.

Council of State Historical Records Coordinators (COSHRC)

www.coshrc.org/arc/states/res_disa.htm

COSHRC is a national organization of state historical records coordinators that encourages cooperation among the states, defines and communicates archival and records concerns at a national level, and works to ensure that the nation's documentary heritage is preserved and accessible. The CSHRC Web site features an Archives Resource Center with a state-by-state list of disaster planning resources.

Disaster Mitigation Planning Assistance

www.matrix.msu.edu/~disaster/

Examples of disaster plans and information on recovery techniques are available on this site, a joint project of the Center for Great Lakes Culture and the Michigan State University Libraries.

Federal Emergency Management Agency (FEMA)

www.fema.gov/ehp

The FEMA Web site section on Environmental & Historic Preservation lists on-line resources including the *Emergency Response and Salvage Wheel* and *Tips for Saving Water-Damaged Photographs, Books and Textiles After the Flood*.

Georgia Department of Archives and History (GDAH)

www.sos.state.ga.us/archives/ps/disaster.htm

The GDAH site includes preservation technical leaflets and disaster recovery and preparedness guidelines, as well as information on the Southeast Regional Conservation Association, which supports disaster-related activities in the Southeast. GDAH also provides information and advice for individuals seeking assistance in salvaging their personal belongings.

Inland Empire Library Disaster Response Network (IELDRN)

www.ieldrn.org

IELDRN is a cooperative network of public and academic libraries in San Bernardino, Riverside, and Eastern Los Angeles Counties that work together to prepare for and recover from disasters. IELDRN offers a model Mutual Aid Agreement, a sample disaster plan, and Web links on library disaster preparedness and library materials conservation.

Library of Congress Preservation Directorate

www.loc.gov/preserv/pubsemer.html

The Library of Congress Preservation Directorate provides links to disaster-related resources including *Emergency Drying Procedures for Water Damaged Collections*, *Emergency Preparedness for Library of Congress Collections*, and *A Primer on Disaster Preparedness, Management and Response: Paper*.

Library Preservation at Harvard

preserve.harvard.edu/emergencies/index.html

This site provides information about emergency response and the salvage of library materials and includes planning templates and salvage information for many types of collections.

Los Angeles Preservation Network (LAPnet)

www.usc.edu/org/LAPnet

LAPnet is a preservation network for archives, libraries, conservators, and records managers in the Los Angeles area. Their web site provides a generic disaster plan, a list of disaster consultants, and local sources for disaster supplies and suppliers.

Minnesota Historical Society

www.mnhs.org/preserve/conservation/emergency.html

The Minnesota Historical Society Web site provides tip sheets detailing salvage measures for materials such as paper, leather, paintings on canvas, textiles and clothing, and wood.

National Archives and Records Administration (NARA)

www.archives.gov/preservation/emergency_preparedness.html

NARA is an independent federal agency that oversees the management of all federal records. On-line resources include *A Primer on Disaster Preparedness, Management and Response: Paper-Based Materials* and *Vital Records and Records Disaster Mitigation and Recovery: An Instructional Guide*.

Northeast Document Conservation Center (NEDCC)

www.nedcc.org/welcome/disaster.htm

The NEDCC is a regional conservation center serving New England as well as New York, New Jersey, Maryland, and Delaware. NEDCC offers an emergency assistance program for institutions and individuals with damaged paper-based collections. On-line Emergency Management Technical Leaflets range from "Emergency Management Suppliers and Services" to "Protecting Collections during Renovation."

Regional Alliance for Preservation (RAP)

www.rap-arcc.org/

RAP serves as a national network for preservation and conservation organizations dedicated to disseminating information and promoting public awareness. An on-line bibliography is searchable by topic and includes a section on emergency preparedness.

San Diego/Imperial County Libraries Disaster Response Network (SILDRN)

orpheus.ucsd.edu/sildrn/

SILDRN is a regional cooperative organization, providing mutual aid in preparing for and coping with disasters affecting libraries. Resources include materials on planning and recovery and information on local suppliers.

SOLINET

www.solinet.net/preservation/

SOLINET is a nonprofit membership organization dedicated to strengthening libraries. The Preservation Field Service Program offers emergency disaster assistance to individuals and institutions and includes group discounts on supplies, leaflets and other publications, videos, and consultations.

The Upper Midwest Conservation Association (UMCA)

www.preserveart.org/fieldservices/fieldservices.html

The UMCA is a regional center working for the preservation and conservation of art and artifacts in the Upper Midwest. The Field Services Department is available during work hours to give immediate assistance with disaster recovery efforts. Assistance in emergency preparedness planning is provided in the form of telephone consultations, on-site visits, and workshops.

In 2003, Hurricane Isabel hit
Colonial National Historical
Park, soaking the archaeological
collections at the Jamestown
Visitor Center in five feet of
water. Objects were dried on
screens after being washed to
remove mold and debris.

Photo courtesy the National Park
Service Museum Resource Center.

About the Sponsors

Before and After Disasters: Federal Funding for Cultural Institutions is an initiative of the Heritage Emergency National Task Force. It was written and produced by Heritage Preservation with funding from and in partnership with the Federal Emergency Management Agency (FEMA) and the National Endowment for the Arts (NEA) as a service to the American cultural community.

The **Heritage Emergency National Task Force** was formed in 1995 to help promote preparedness and mitigation measures and provide expert information on response and salvage. Sponsored by FEMA and Heritage Preservation, the Task Force works to help libraries, archives, museums, and historic sites safeguard their collections. The Task Force is a partnership of 36 national organizations and federal agencies that brings to its programs a nationwide network of expertise. Its best-known disaster resource, the *Emergency Response and Salvage Wheel*, is used by cultural institutions around the world and has been translated into six languages.

The **Federal Emergency Management Agency** became part of the U.S. Department of Homeland Security on March 1, 2003. FEMA's continuing mission within the new department is to lead the effort to prepare the nation for all hazards and effectively manage federal response and recovery efforts following any national incident. FEMA also initiates proactive mitigation activities, trains first responders, and manages the National Flood Insurance Program.

The **National Endowment for the Arts** is the largest annual funder of the arts in the United States. An independent federal agency, the NEA is the official arts organization of the United States government, dedicated to supporting excellence in the arts, both new and established; bringing the arts to all Americans; and providing leadership in arts education.

Heritage Preservation is a national nonprofit advocate and resource for the proper care of works of art, books and archives, documents and photographs, architecture and monuments, natural science specimens, and family heirlooms.

Further information on *Before and After Disasters* and a PDF version of the publication are available at www.heritageemergency.org. Printed copies can also be ordered at no cost from the FEMA Distribution Center. To place an order, please call (800) 480-2520.

Designed by Fletcher Design, Inc./Washington, DC

Heritage Preservation

The National Institute for Conservation

1012 14th St. NW, Suite 1200
Washington, DC 20005
202-233-0800

www.heritagepreservation.org

Heritage
Emergency
National Task Force